Fuck That Shit

SWEAR WORD COLORING BOOK

The Universe Adult Coloring Book featured with beautiful geometry

By

Florence Clark

Happy Coloring!

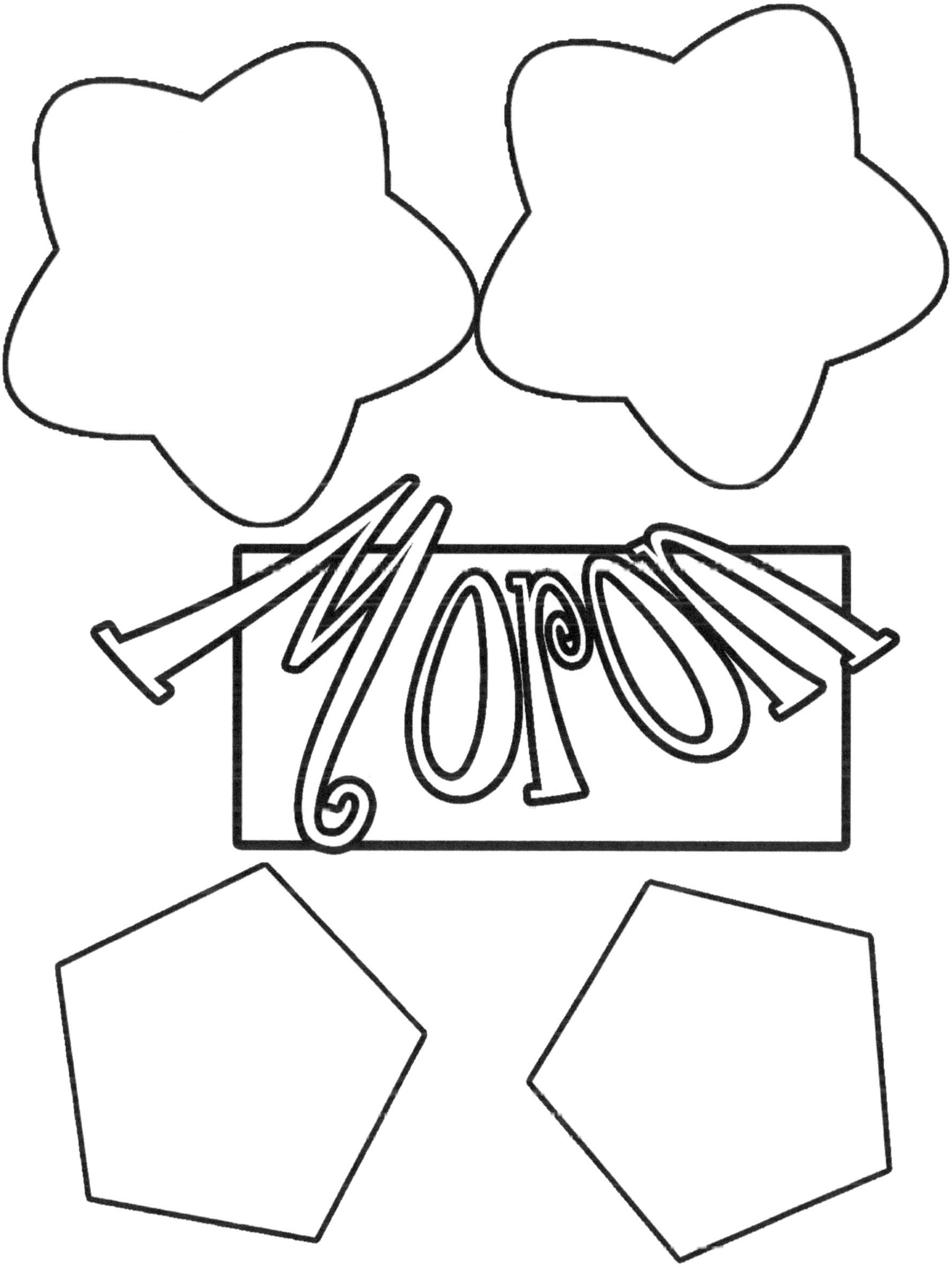

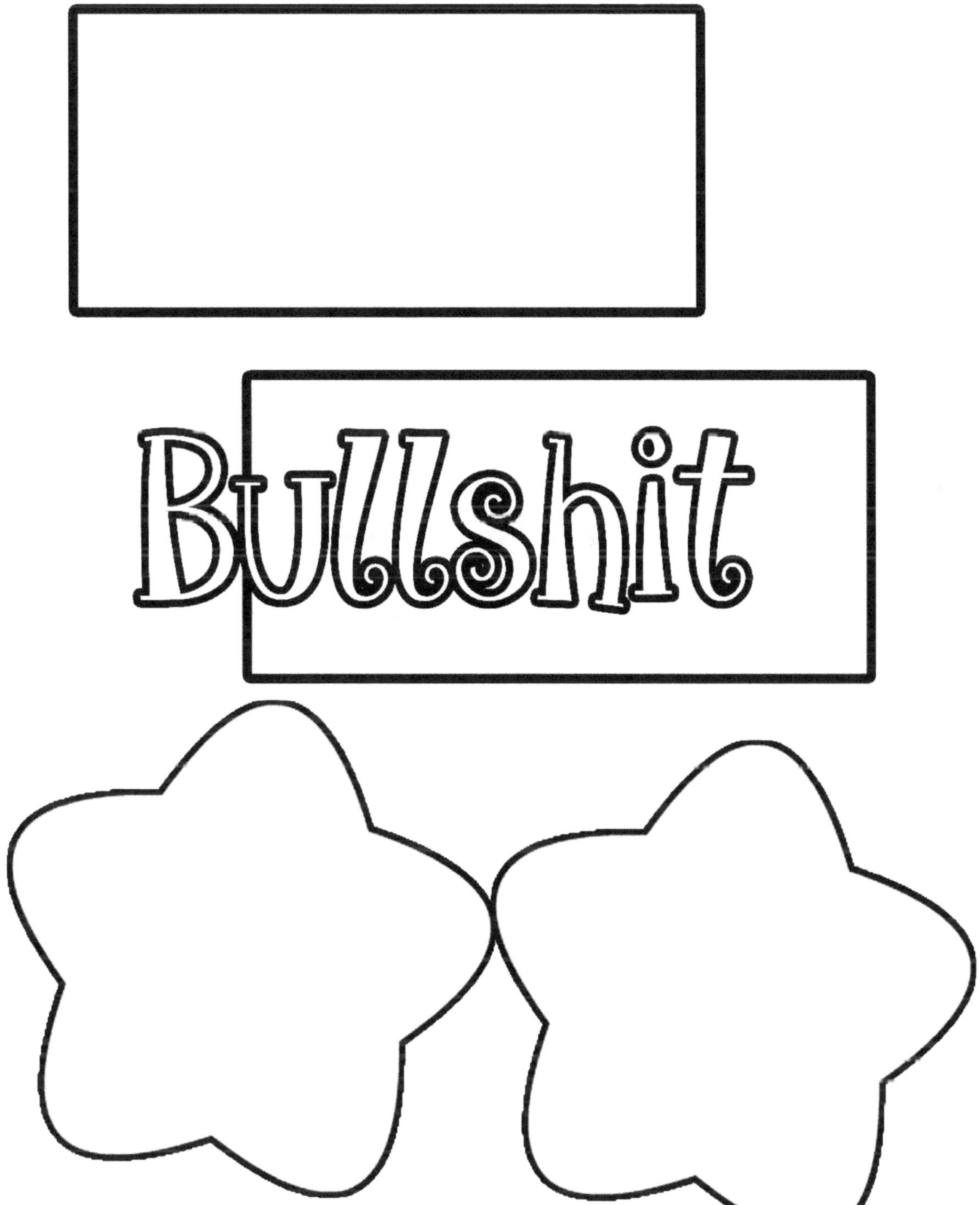
Bullshit

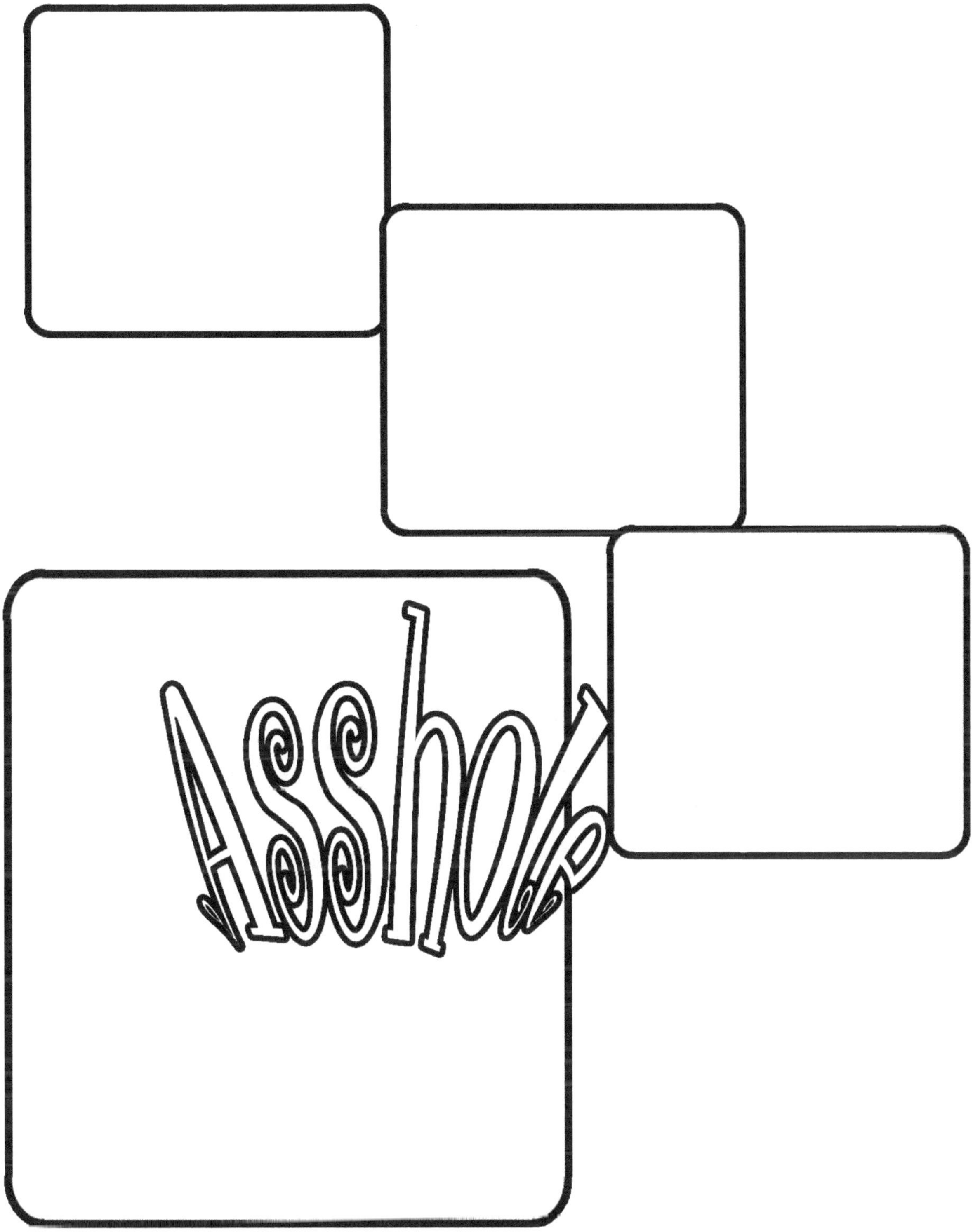
Assho

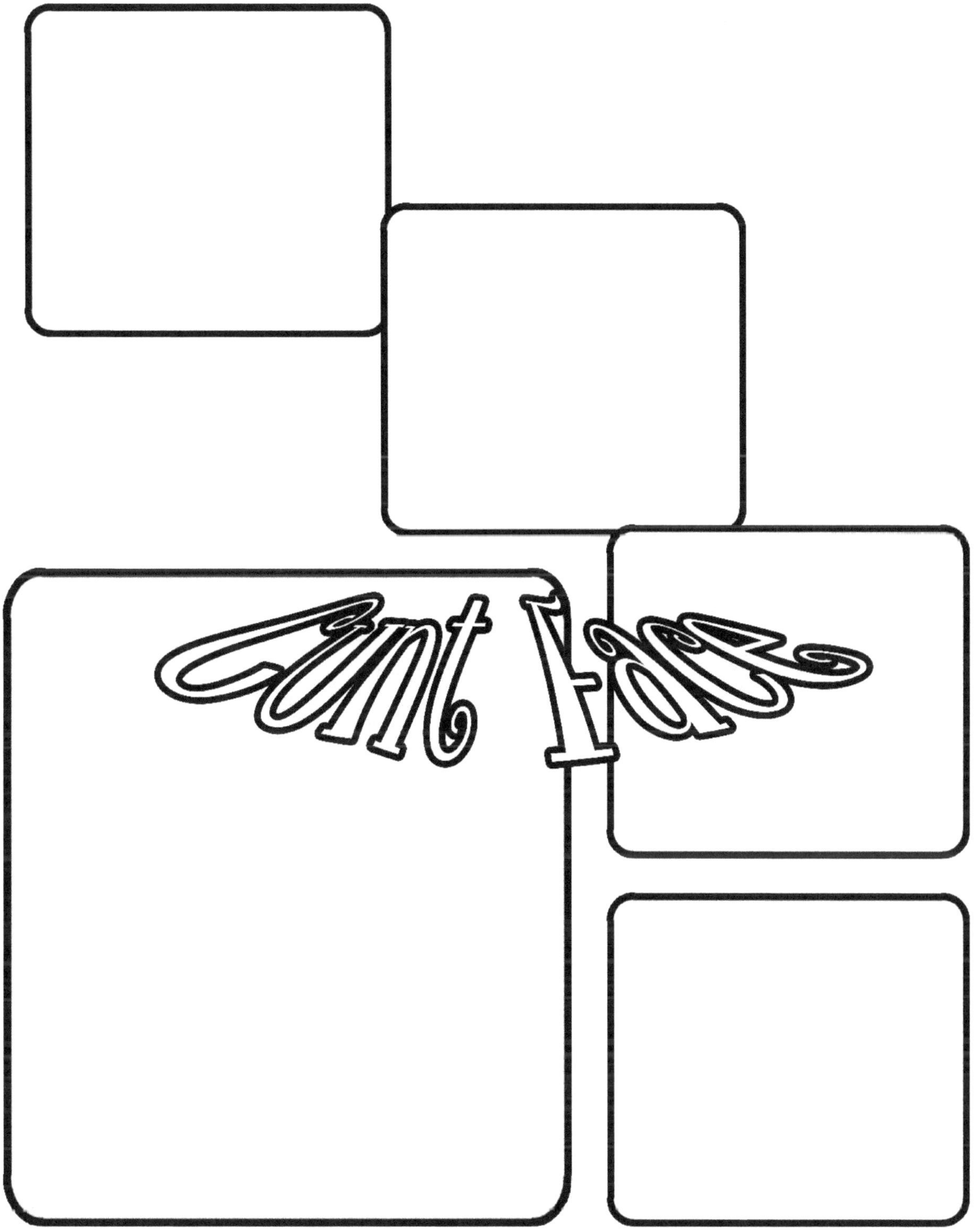

Cock & Balls

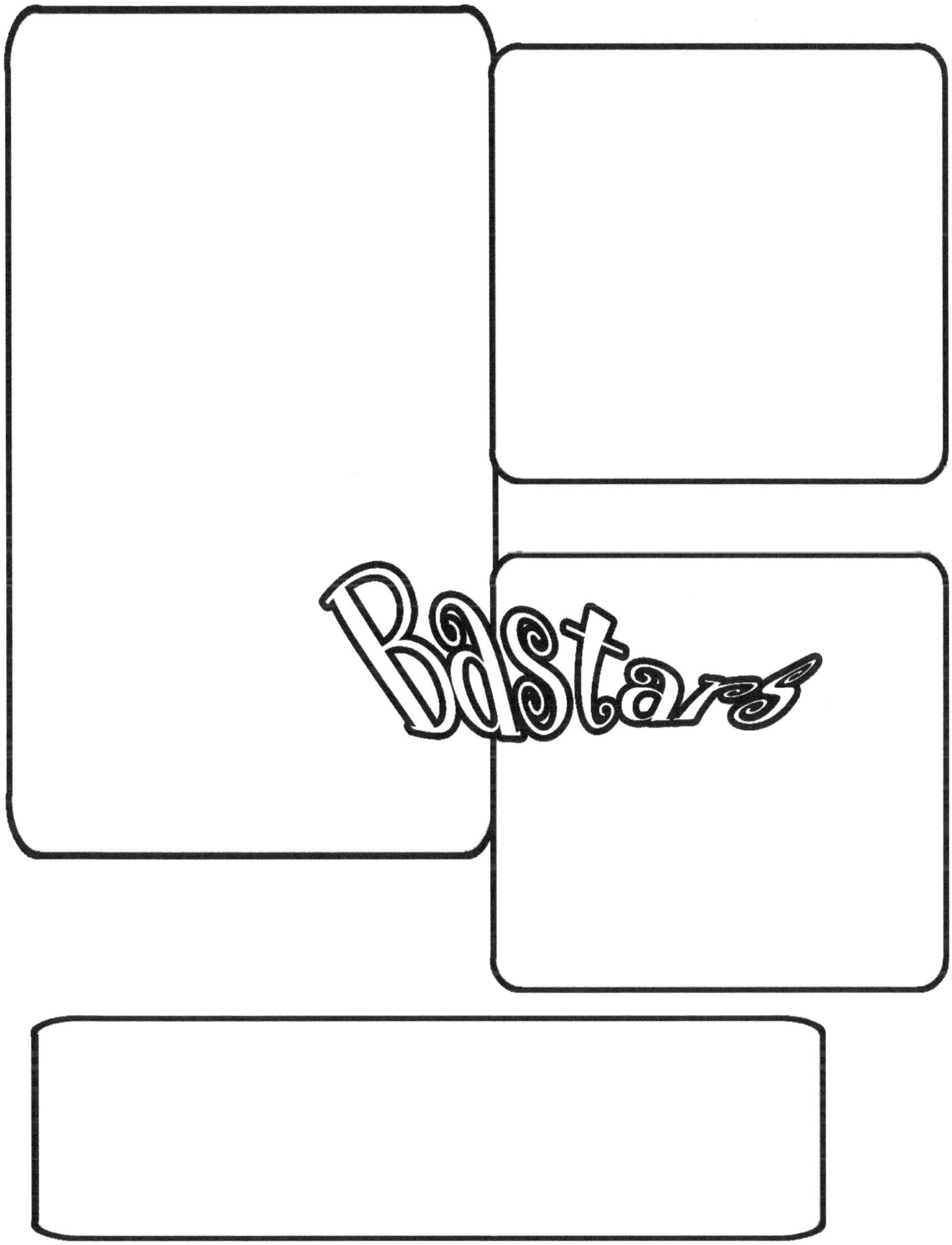
Bastars

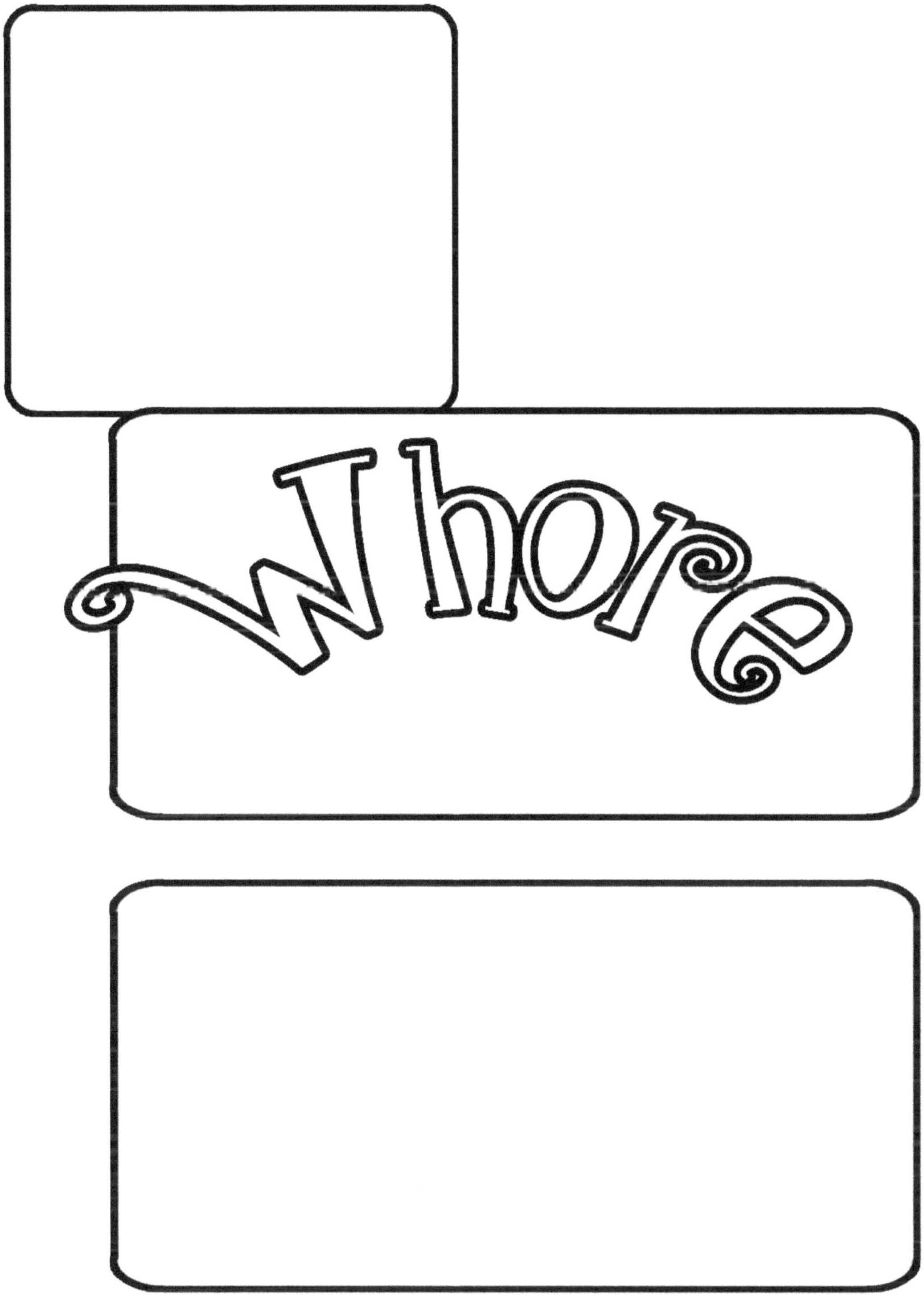
Whore

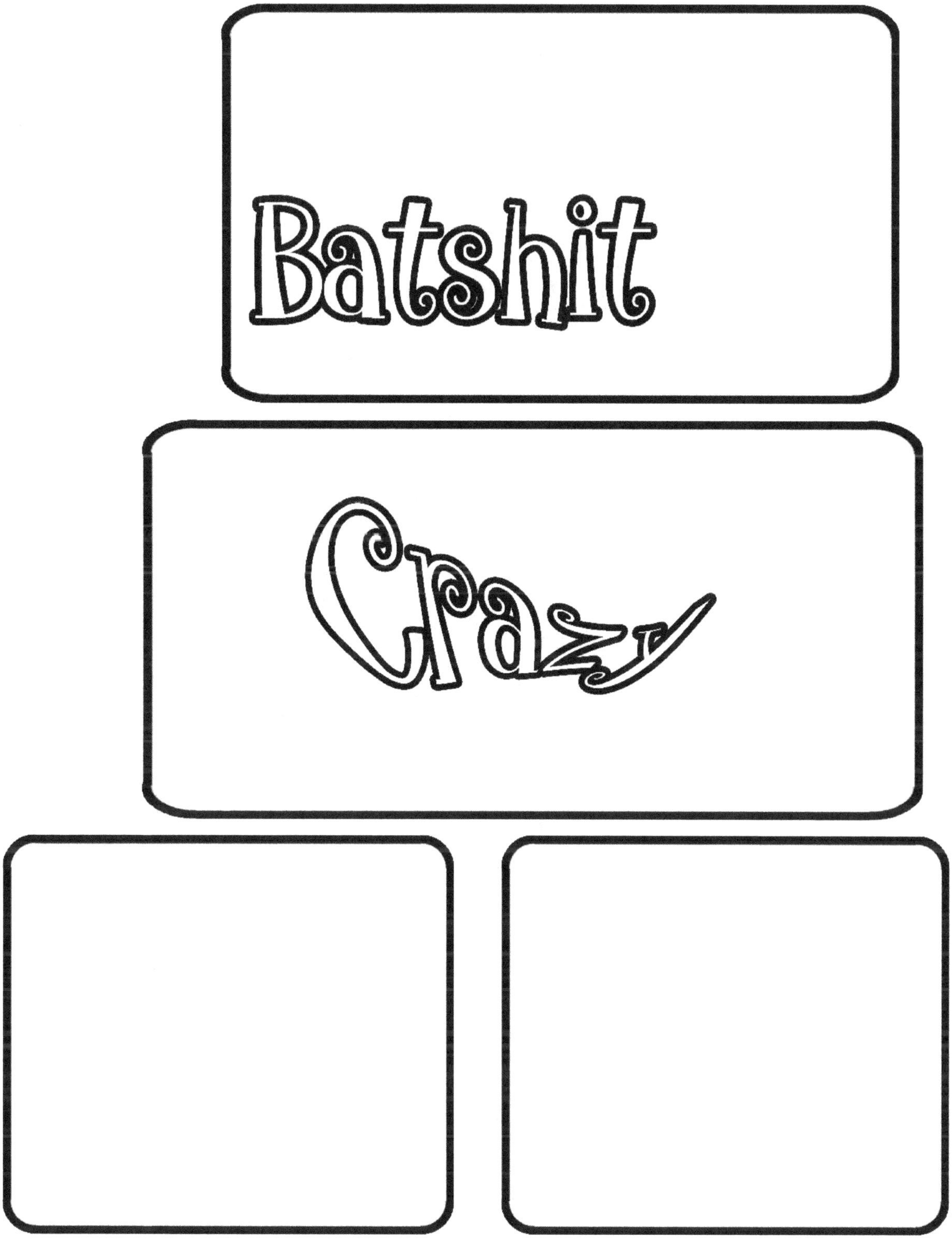
Batshit
Crazy

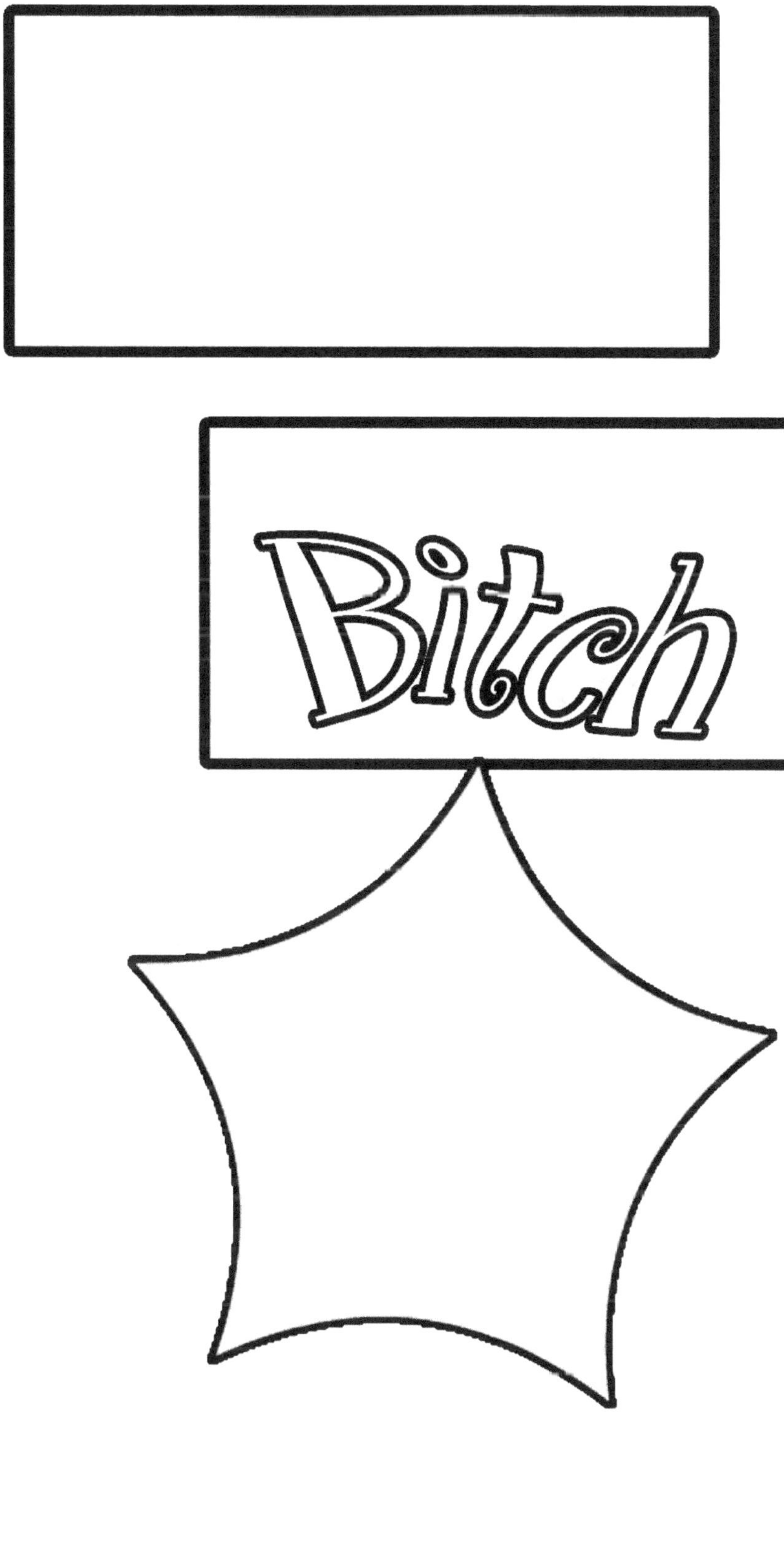
Bitch

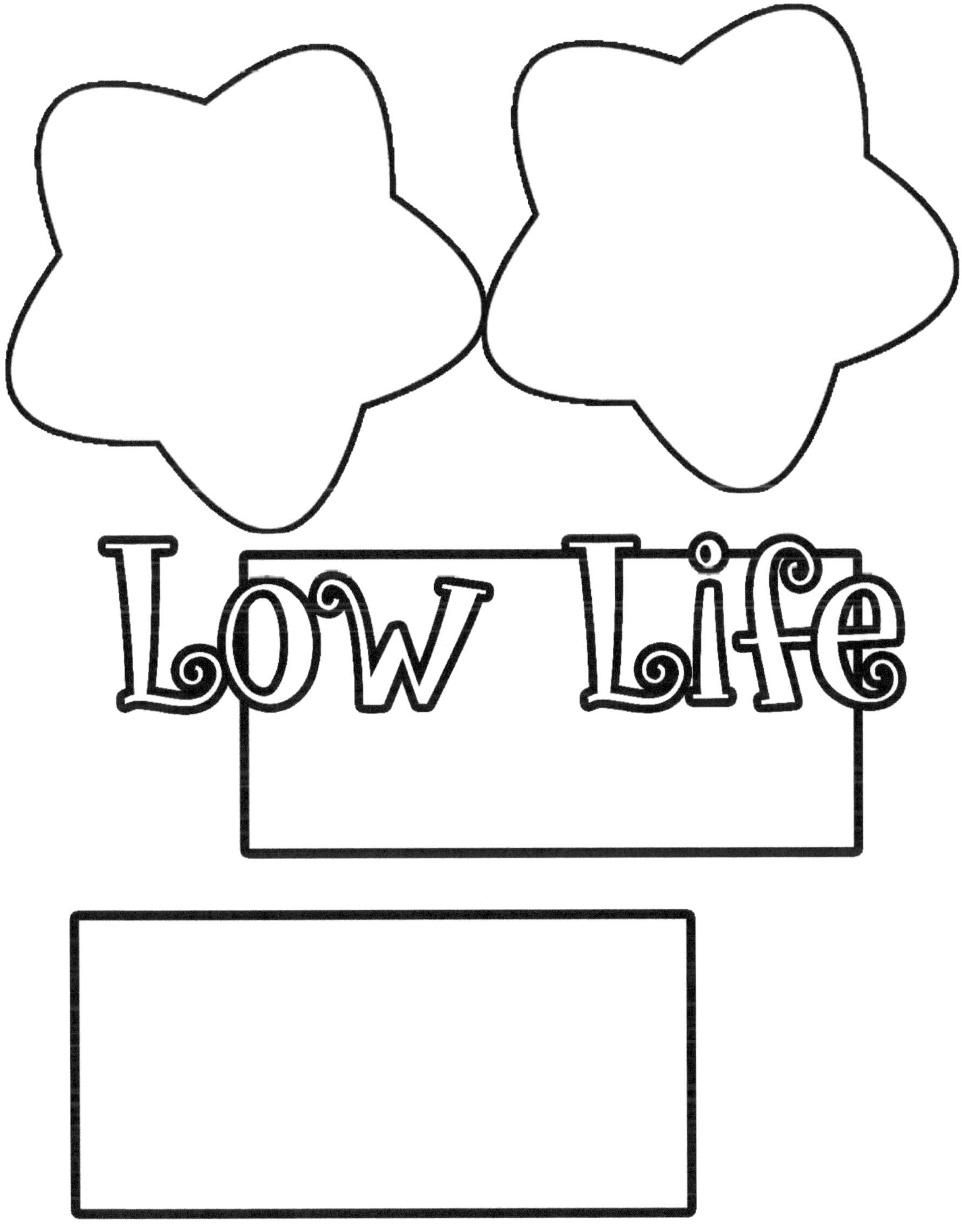
Low Life

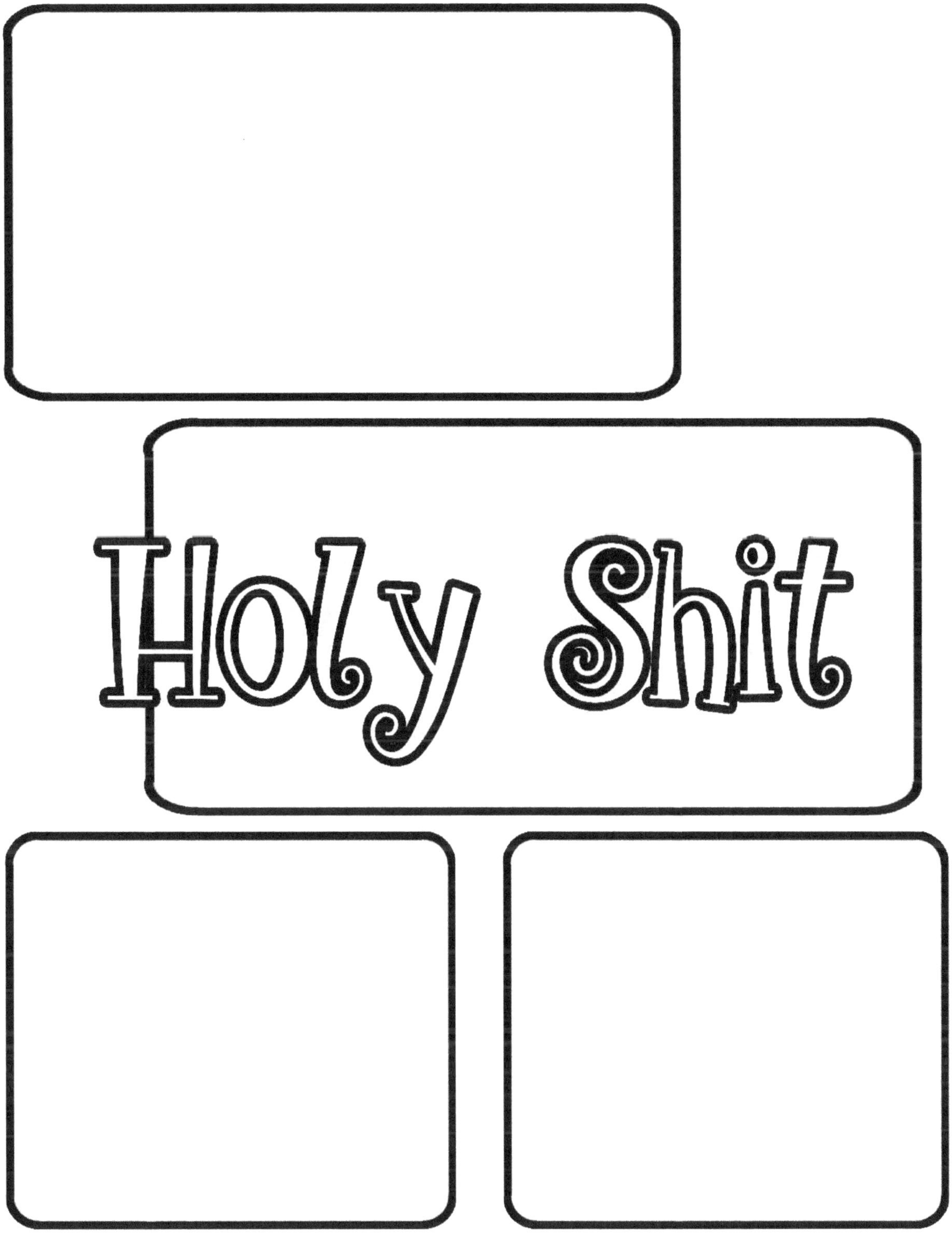
Holy Shit

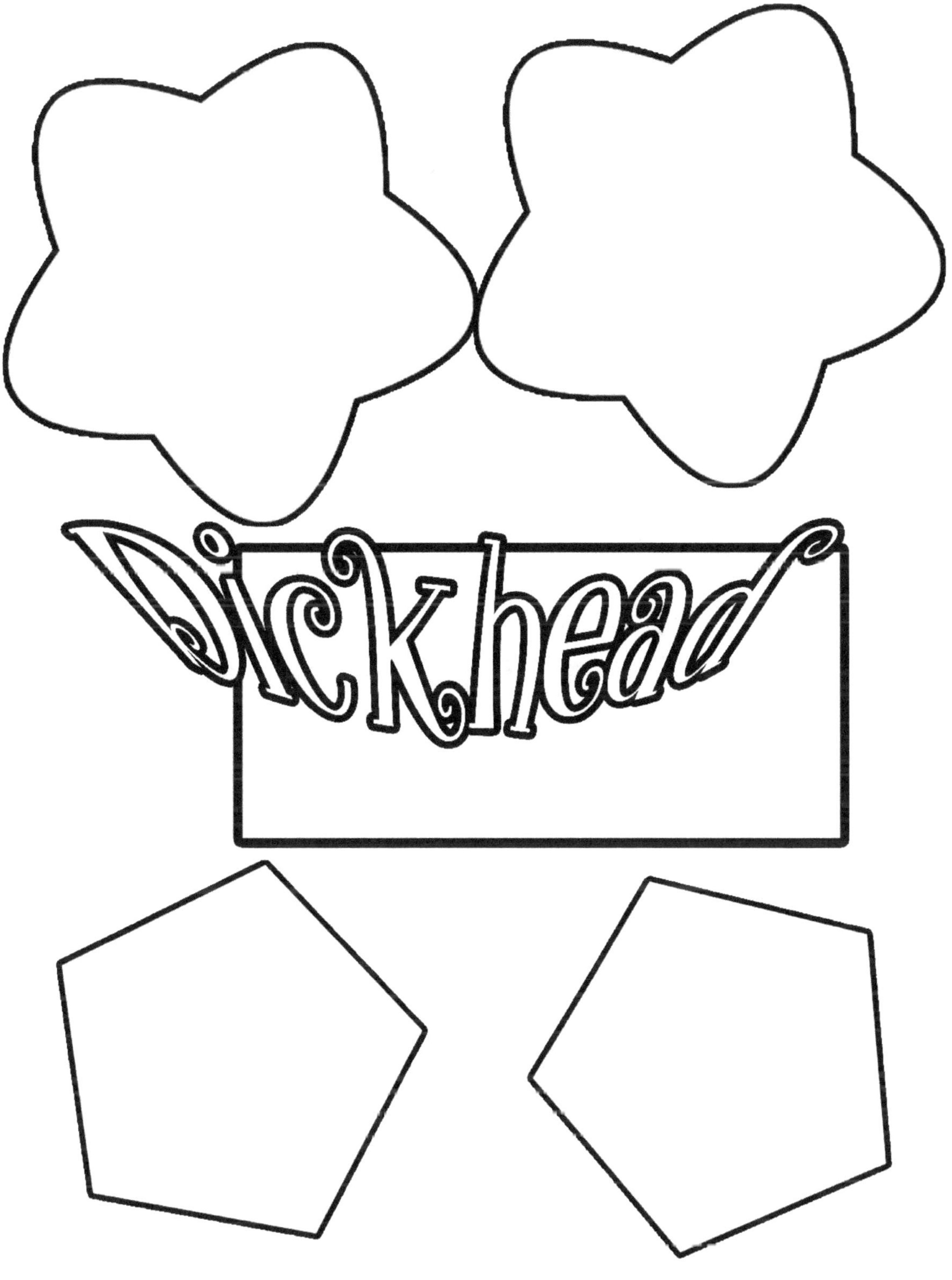
Dickhead

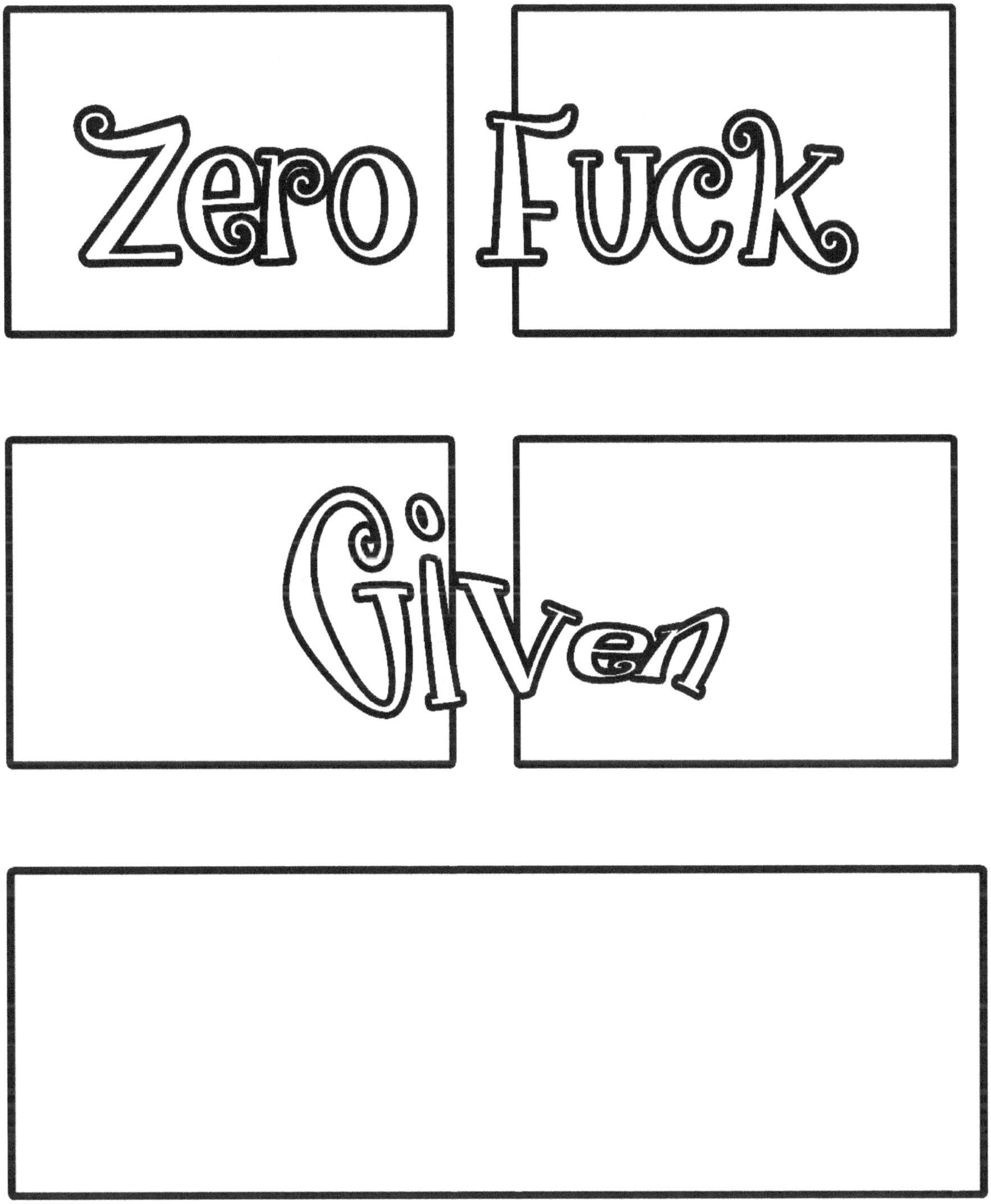
Zero Fuck
Given

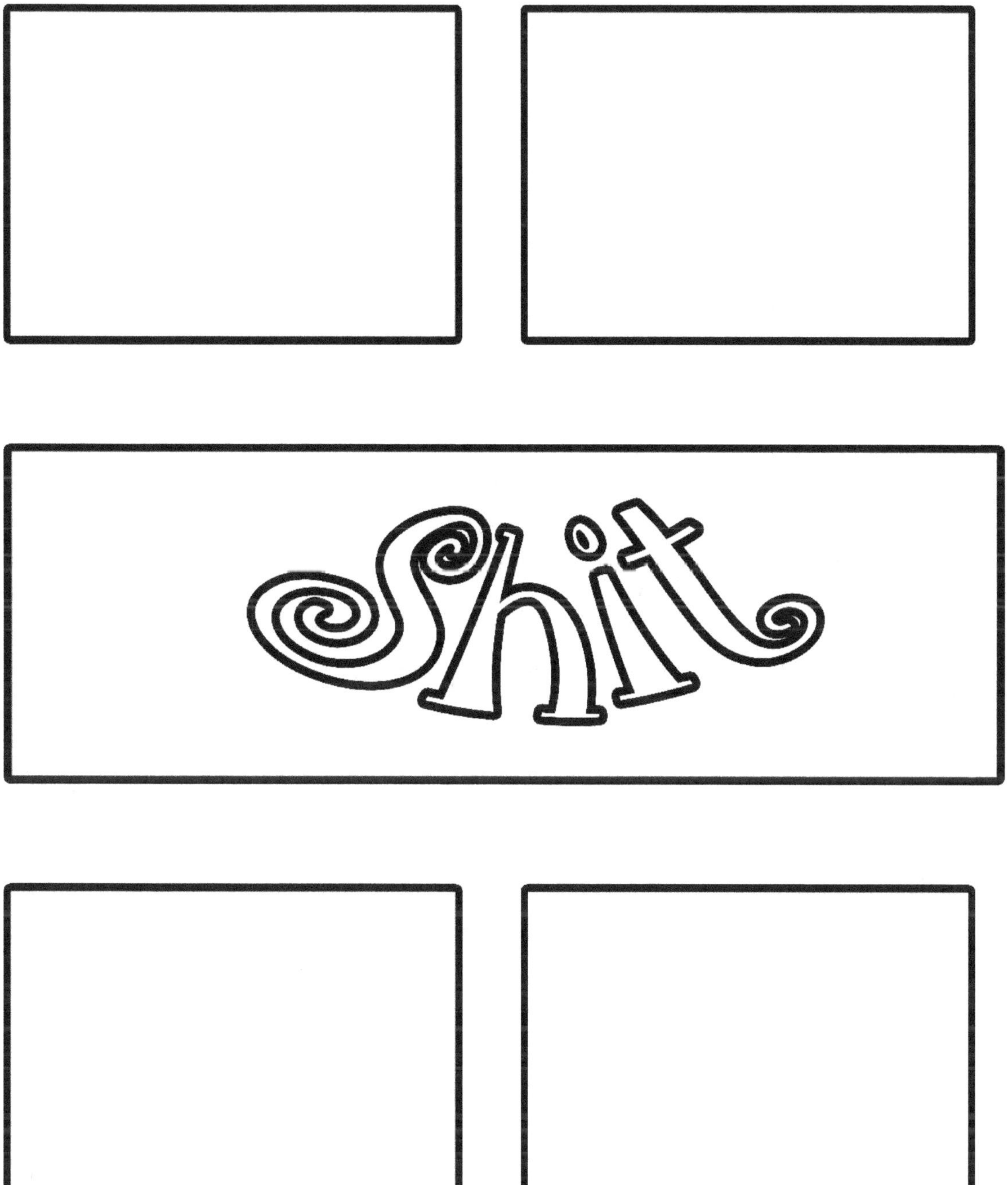
Shit

Ugly big shoes

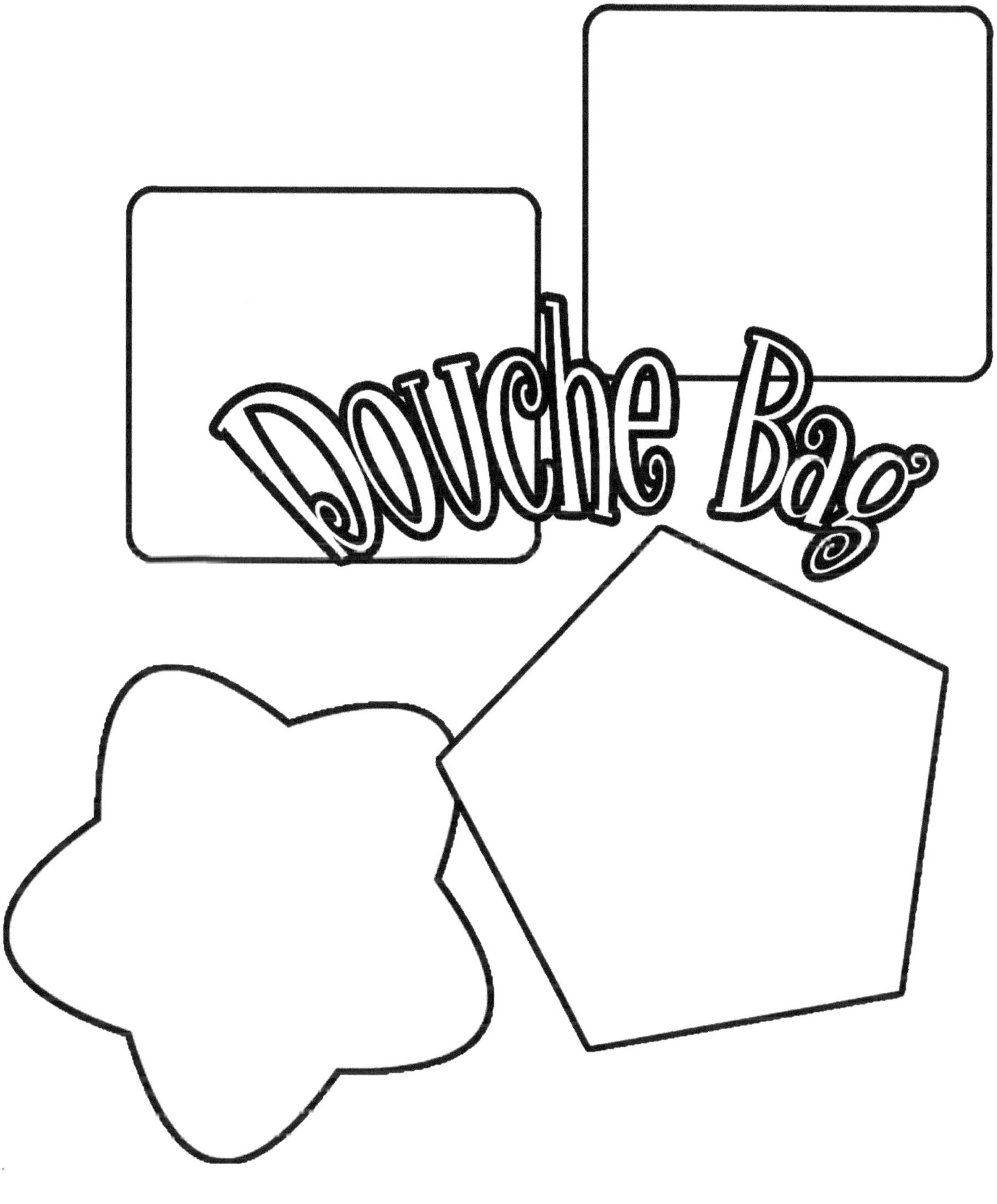
Douche Bag

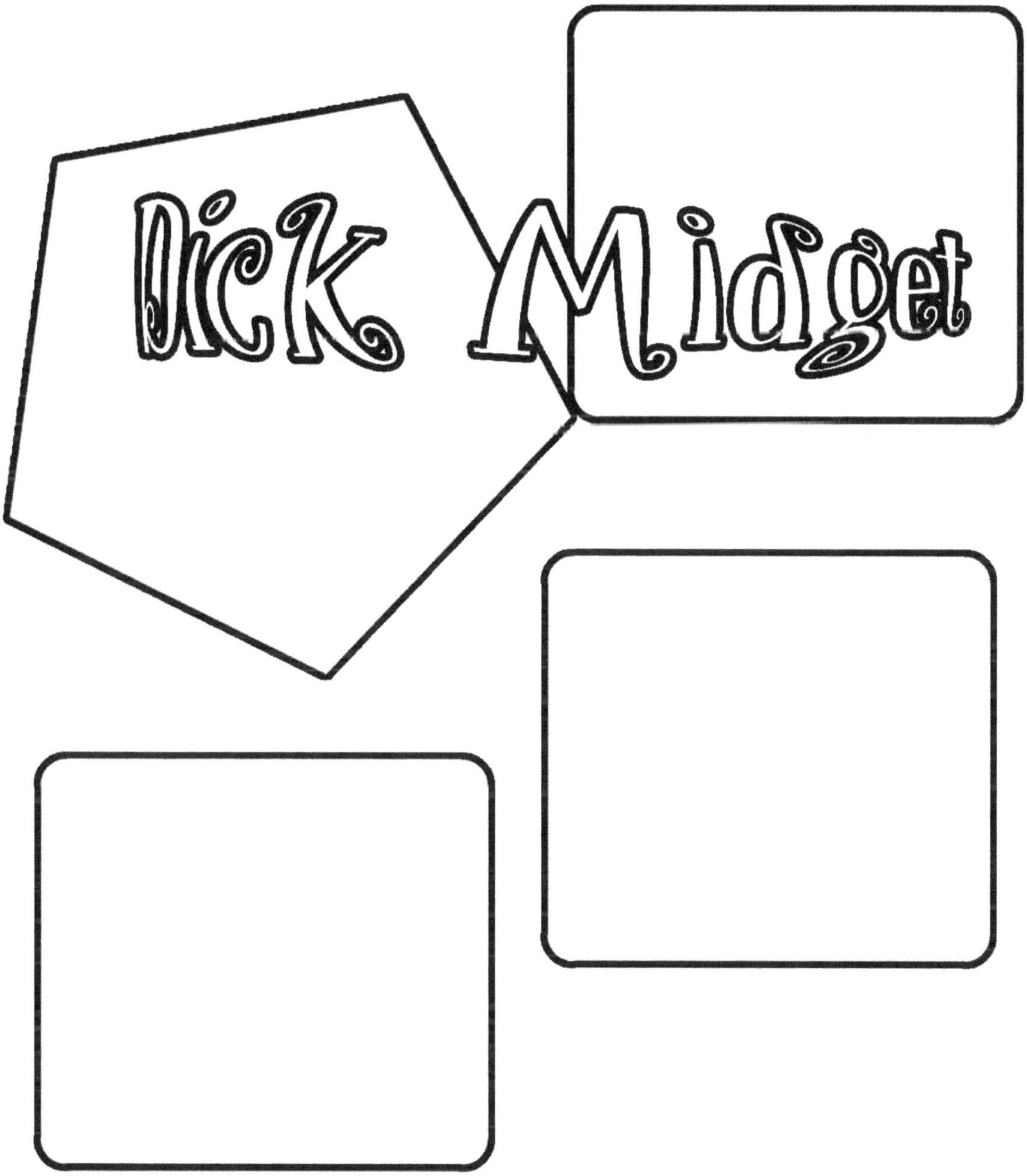
Dick Midget

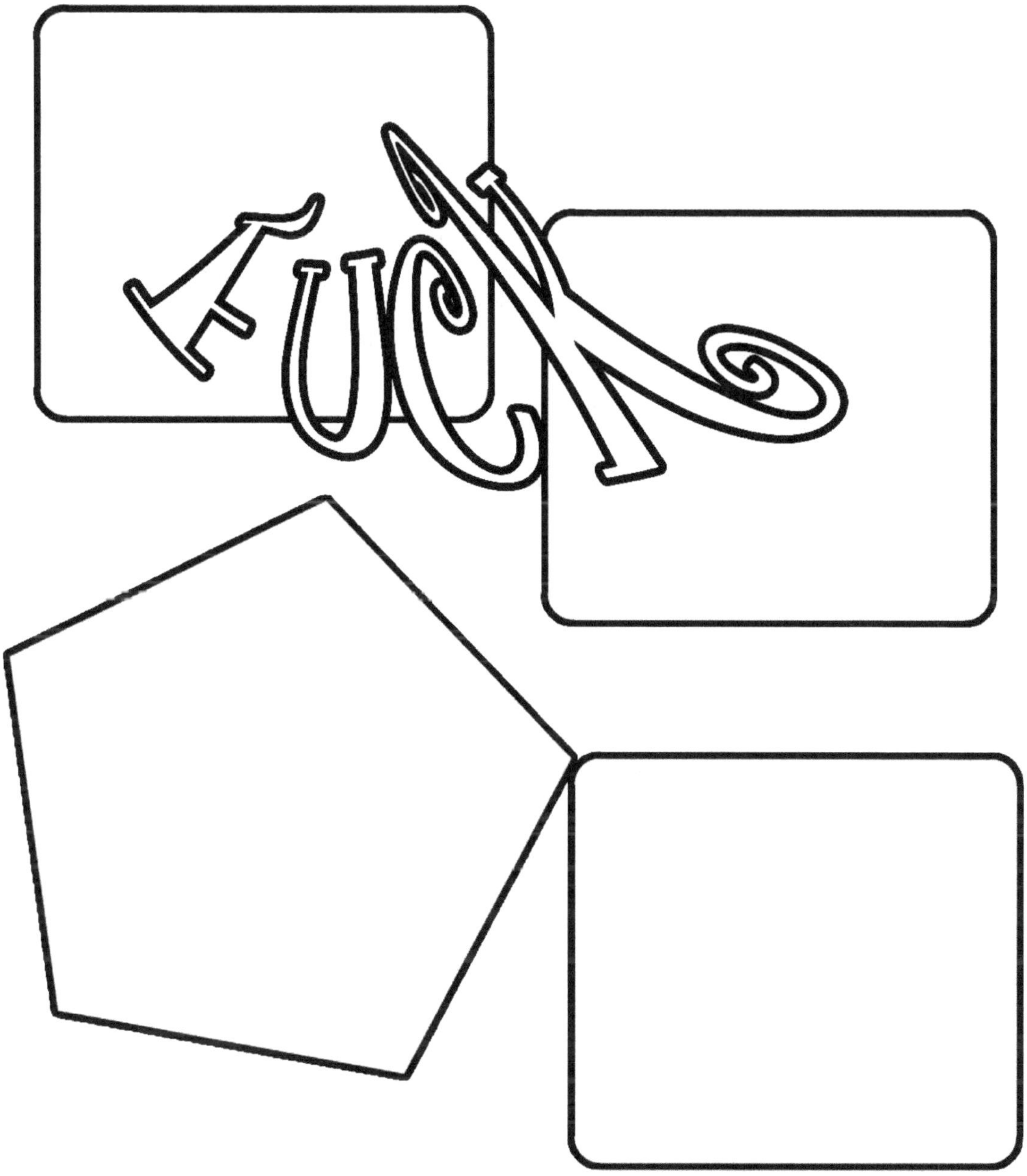
FUCK

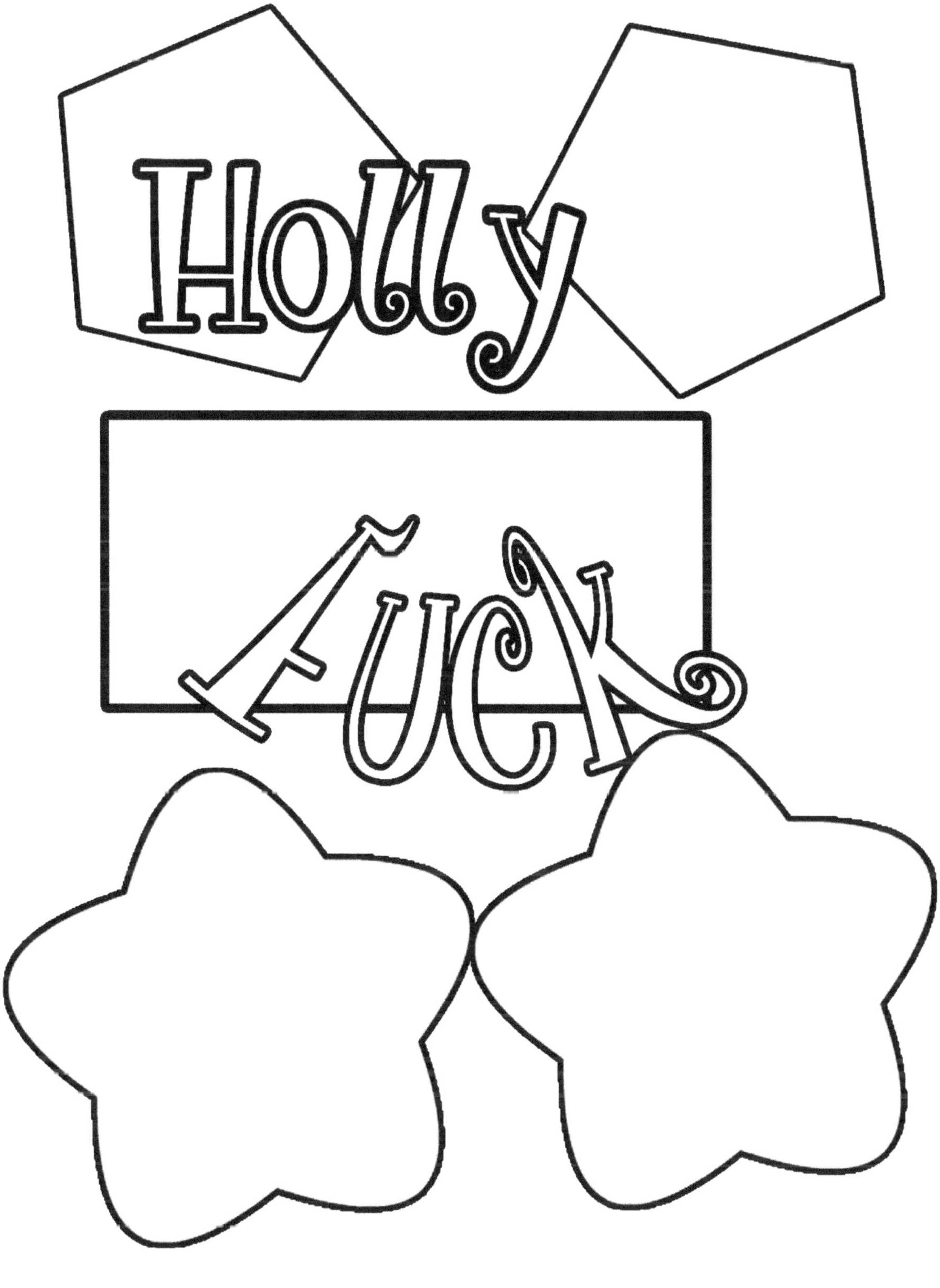
Holly
Fuck

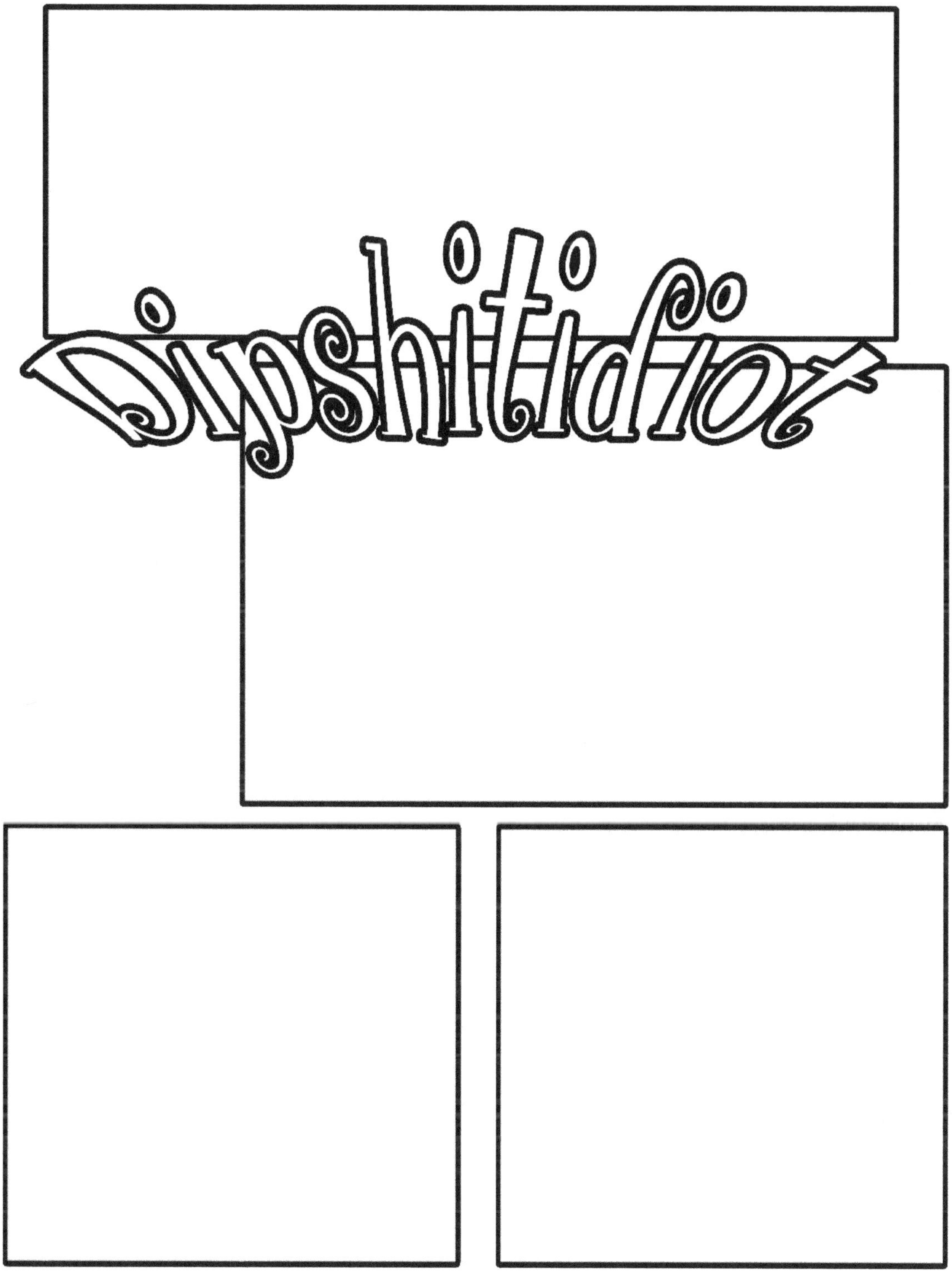
Dipshitidiot

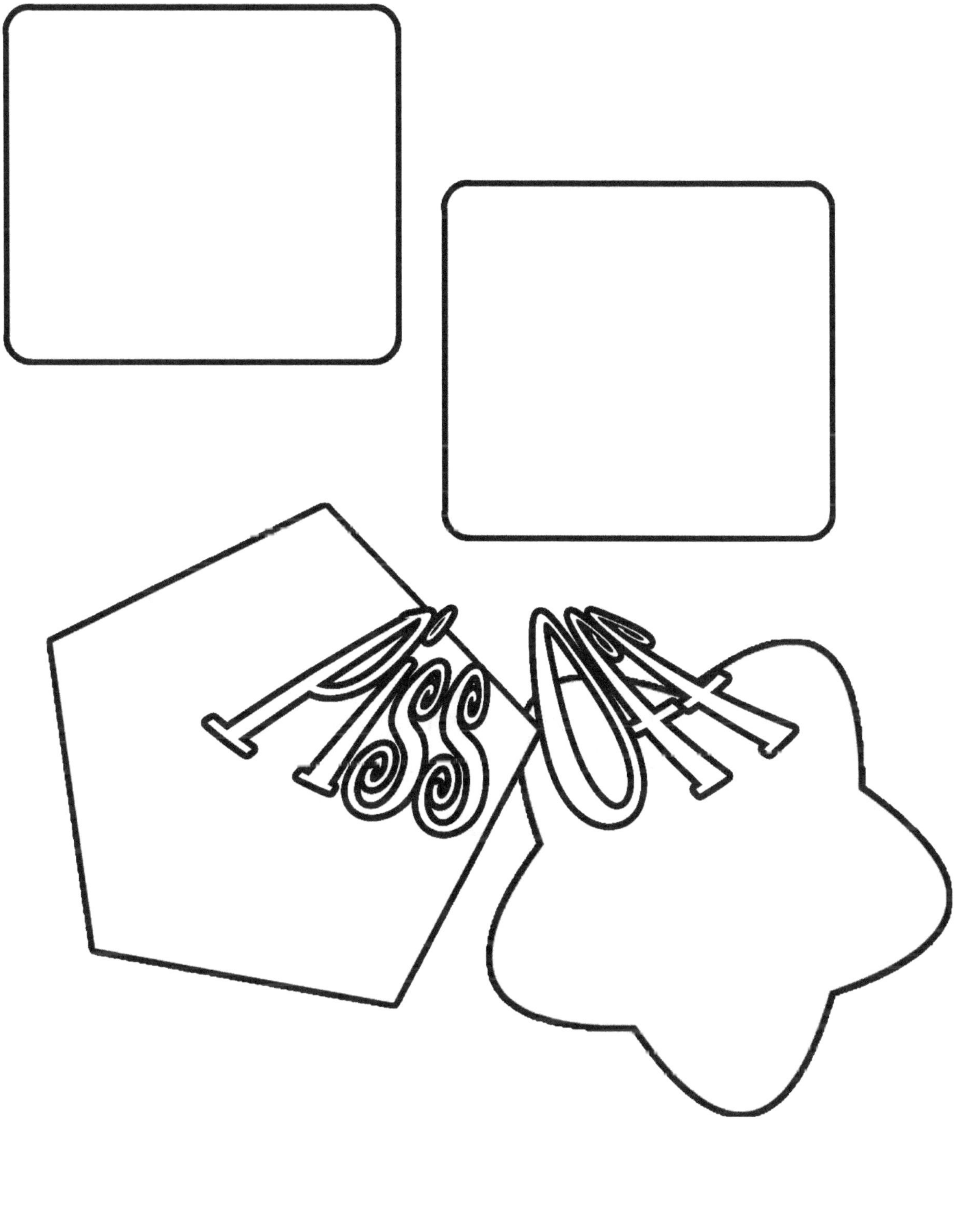

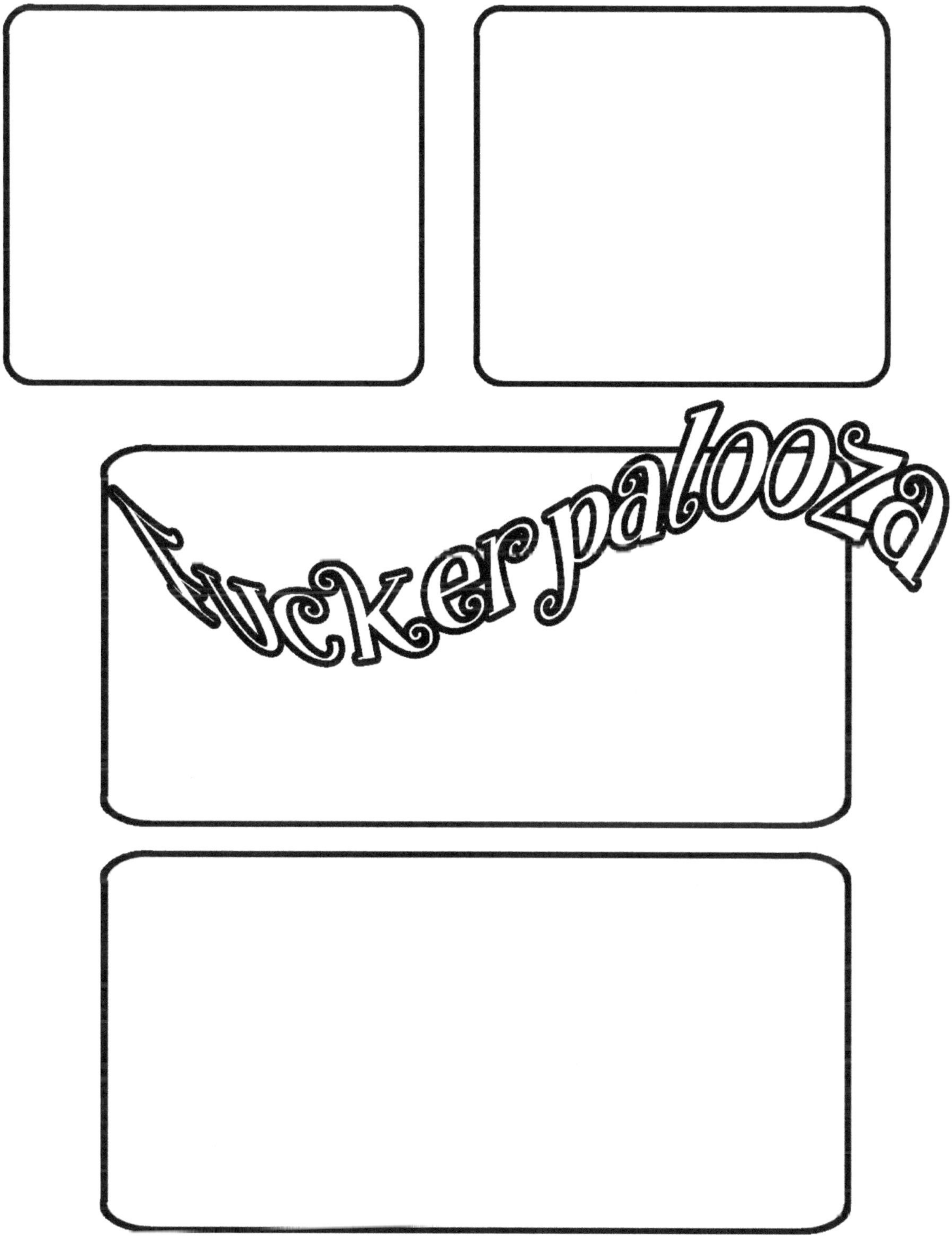
Tuckerpalooza

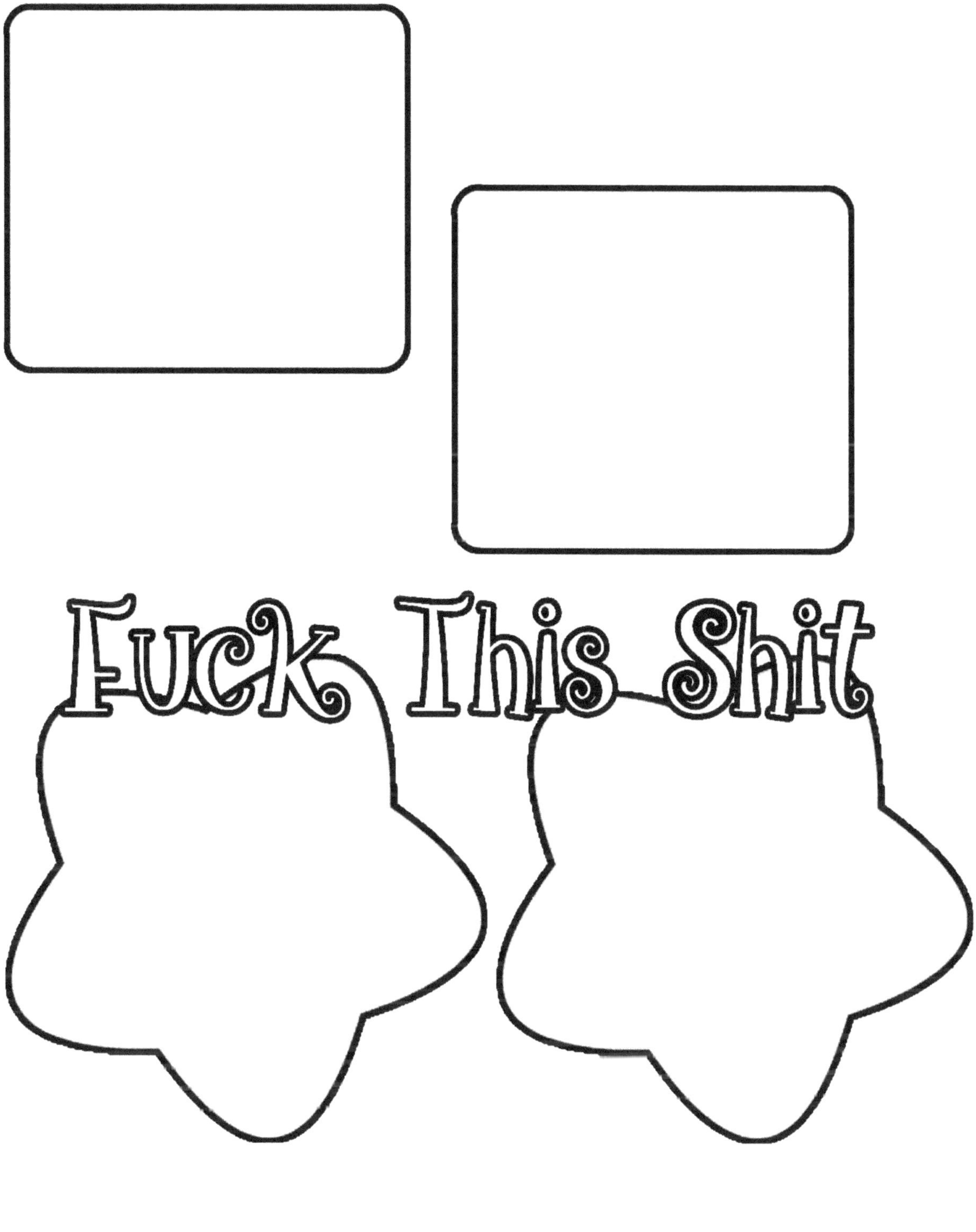
Fuck This Shit

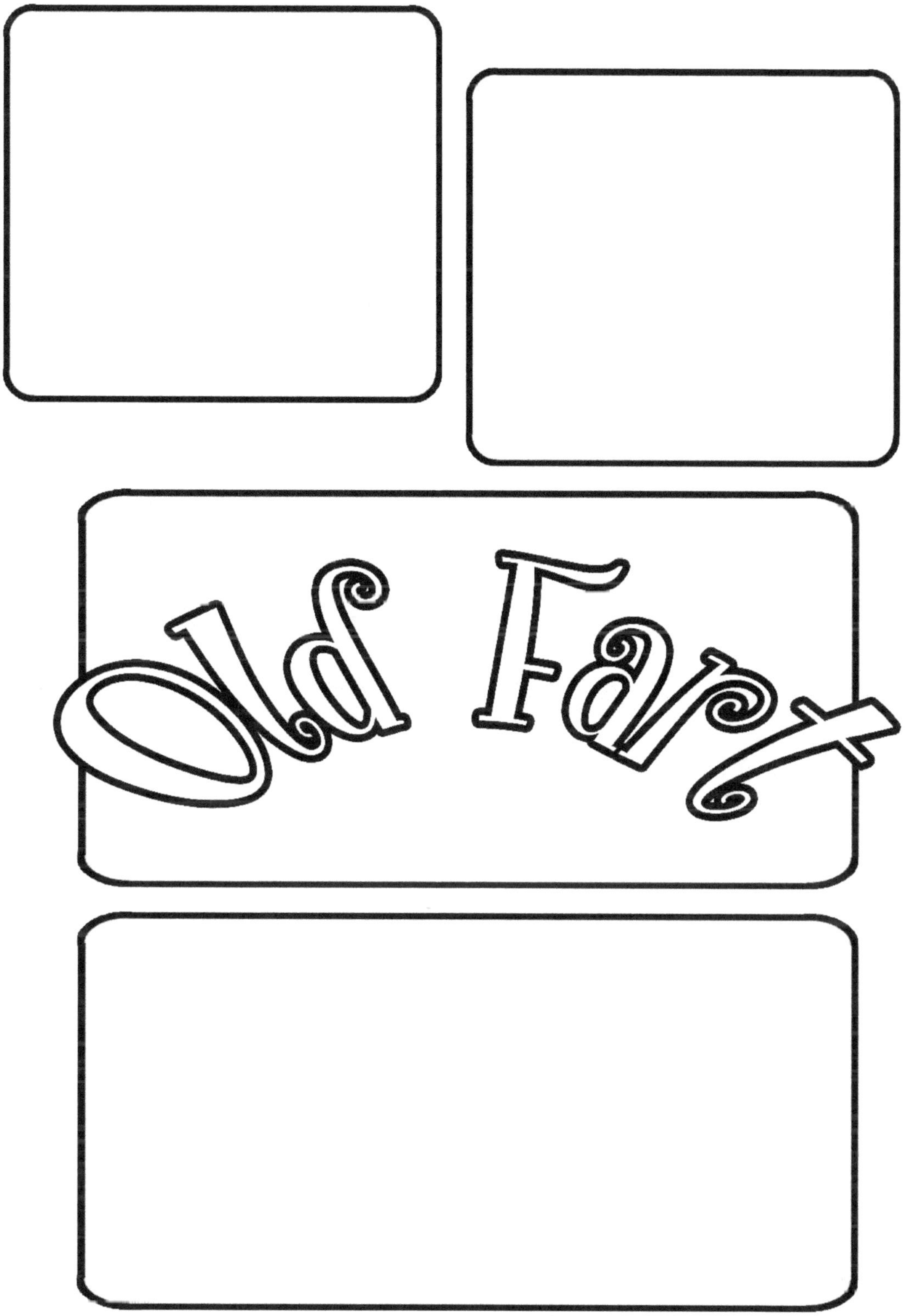
Old Fart

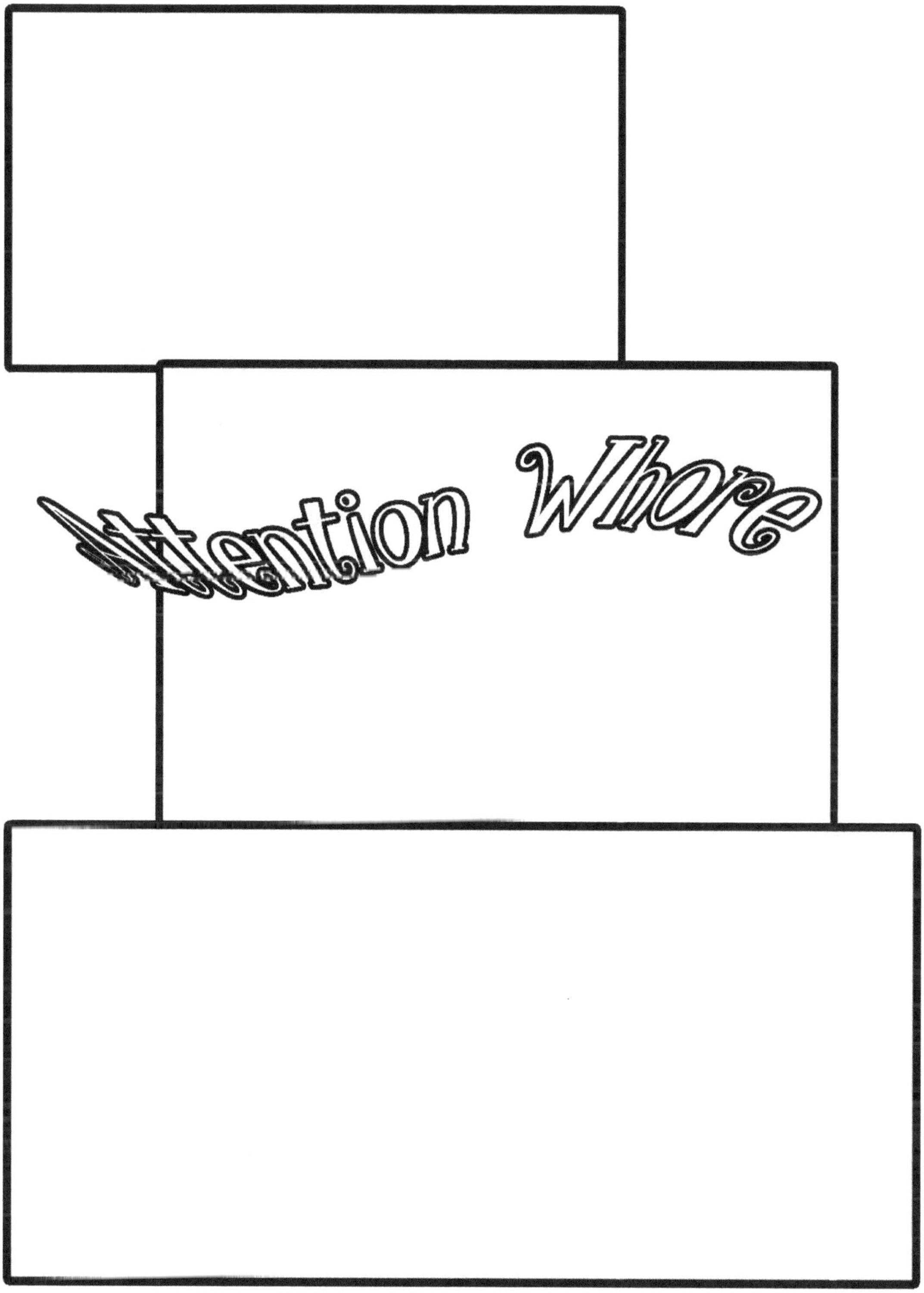
Attention Whore

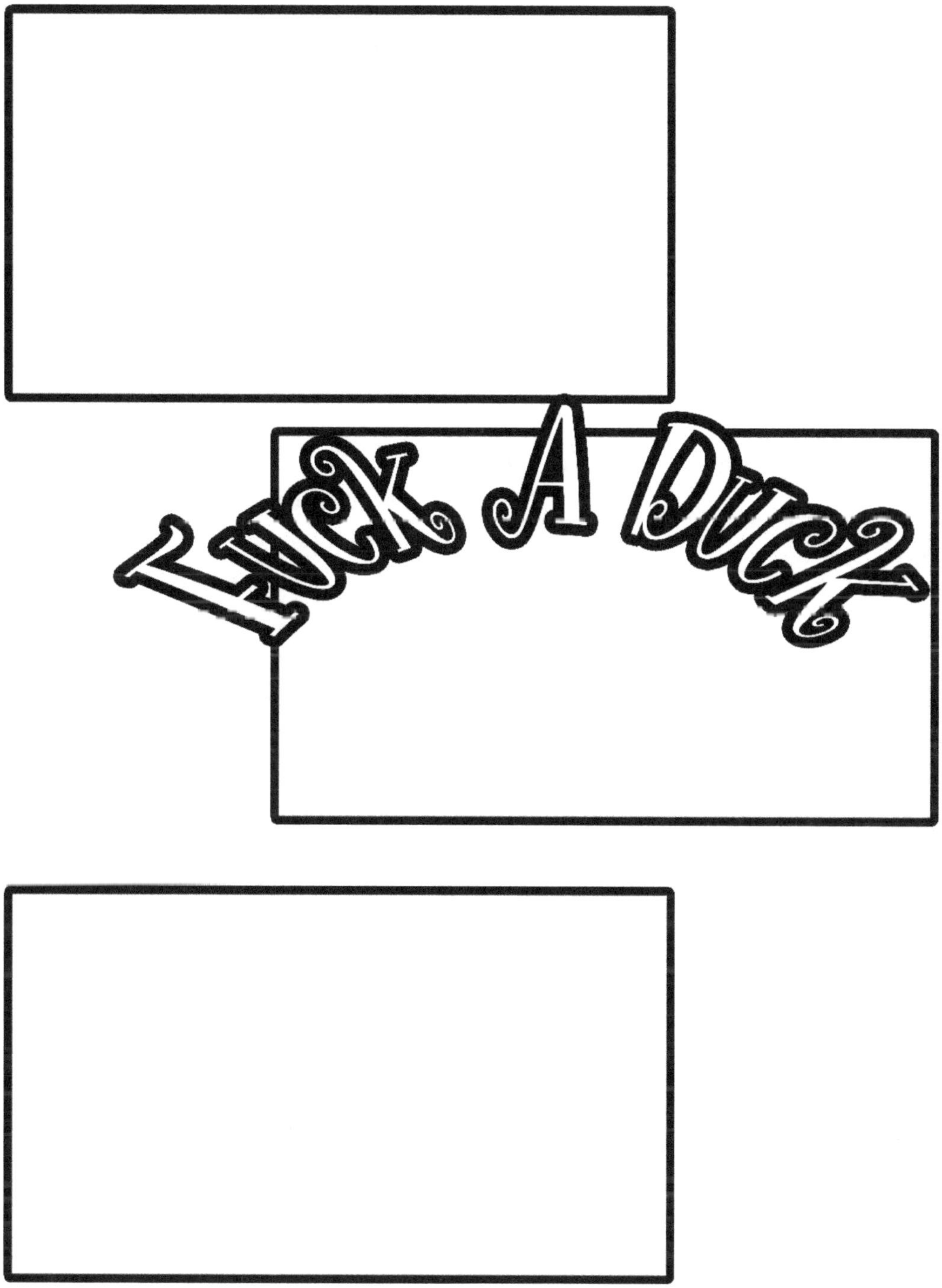
LUCK A DUCK

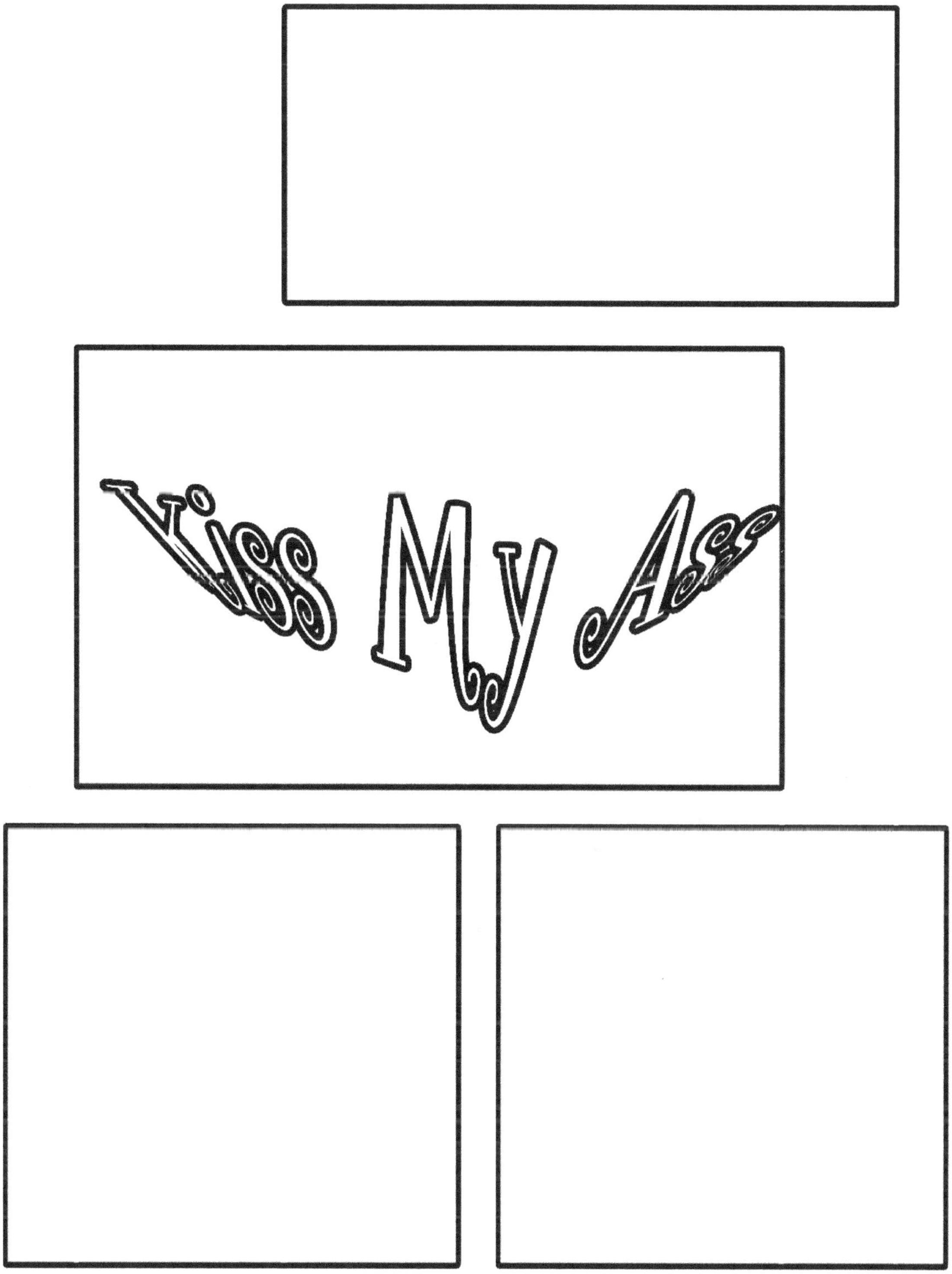
Kiss My Ass

www.ingramcontent.com/pod-product-compliance
Lightning Source LLC
Chambersburg PA
CBHW081125180526
45170CB00008B/3014